After Rain

After Rain

GARY SCHROEDER

— Gary Schroeder —

calligraphy by JS GRAUSTEIN

foreword by JOSEPH HUTCHISON

6 February 2018

Enjoy the blessings of the present moment!

Gary

Folded Word

Meredith, New Hampshire

ISBN: 978-1-61019-240-8

Folded Word
79 Tracy Way
Meredith, NH 03253
United States of America
WWW.FOLDEDWORD.COM

Calligrapher portrait by Michelle Goodearl

98765432 FIRST PRINTING

This one is for Mitchell and Mikayla
for all the joy you have brought into my life.

—

CONTENTS

FOREWORD

In the preface to his anthology *Haiku Seasons: Poetry of the Natural World*, Willilam J. Higginson nutshells the purpose of writing haiku:

> A haiku is the expression (or record) of a moment in which something happened involving the author's perception of nature. There is a connection, a link, between the human and the other.

Certainly the great 17th-century Japanese poet Basho, who essentially invented the kind of poem we think of as haiku today, held this view; he nutshelled it even further, calling the essence of haiku "the heart's immediacy."

It helps, of course, if the poet is conversant with both the world and his or her own heart. In this, Gary Schroeder is a master. He uses words to point us toward what is beyond words and so gives voice to what typically passes without notice. His habit of attention makes these poems fresh and lively, like all experiences we have when we're truly awake. They are gifts, for which gratitude can be the only appropriate response.

~ Joseph Hutchison
Colorado Poet Laureate
(2014–2018)

ACKNOWLEDGEMENTS

The author thanks the editors of the journals that supported his work by publishing previous versions of the following haiku:

- "midway through winter," *2015 Haiku Society of America Members' Anthology*
- "full moon," *2007 Haiku Society of America Members' Anthology*
- "the night rain," *The Heron's Nest*, December 2015
- "the morning after," *Acorn*, Fall 2015
- "almost summers' end," *2010 Haiku Society of America Members' Anthology*

The author, calligrapher, and publisher also thank Barbara Flaherty for expediting the publication of this book through her editorial efforts, as well as Rose Auslander, Casey Tingle, Zakariah Johnson, Kristine Slentz, Sarah Gibson, Claire Graustein, and Kurt Graustein for their assistance at the press during its production.

After Rain

wanting
   to be whole
      the waxing moon

"

full moon
over new fallen snow ~
the night glowing

III

a book of poems —
the day
breaks open

IV

midway through winter
no one in the canyon
water under ice

ν

last year's berries
still linger
on the juniper

VI

walking the fence line
no movement
    in the meadow ~
creek water whispers

VII

after the storm
a chorus of birds
in the aspen grove

VIII

baby mouse
warming by the fire
a posture of prayer

IX

no longer home
her scent still lingers
in the hall closet—

x

surprised
by morning light
in the aspen grove

XI

yet another

spring rain ～

your silence

XII

frogs all night long—
three days of rain
so now they carry on

XIII

morning fog
the heron
      turns its head

a long look back

XIV

no rooster today ~
instead a donkey
            tells me

morning is coming

xv

message sent ~

waiting

for her reply

XVI

another new nest ☙

the house finch
          pauses briefly

so much left to do

XVII

the night rain
one more dream
I don't remember

XVIII

morning fog
    at the edge
of last night's dream

XIX

cricket singing solo
wish
I knew the words

x x

Sunday morning
the eloquent sermon
of a house finch

XXI

a dark-eyed junco
resting on the
          piñon limb
ruffles its feathers

XXII

April morning
and the fleeting
scent
of wild plum

XXIII

morning prayer
in a cathedral
of trees

XXIV

great blue heron
drops a feather
at my feet

xxv

the morning after
an evening rain ~
creek water sings

XXVI

june bug
　　belly up ~
must be july

XXVII

a single bird

singing

in the aspen grove

XXVIII

July's mid-day heat—
the crow in the
            pine tree
changes its tune

XXIX

almost summer's end ~
scrub jay moves
              from post to post
the wind along the ridge

$$x \, x \, x$$

cicadas
in the cottonwoods ==
music for the harvest

XXXI

October evening walk
today
shorter than yesterday

XXXII

.

after rain
the dirt road travels
on my shoes

About the Author

GARY SCHROEDER is the author of four books of poetry, *The Slender Name, Mistaken Lights, Adjacent Solitudes* and *Cricket in the House: A Year's Haiku.* His poems have appeared in a number of journals including *North Dakota Quarterly, The Eleventh Muse, The Bloomsbury Review, Kansas Quarterly, Poetry-North Review, Pendragon, Riverstone, Sackbut Review, Santa Fe Poetry, Soundings East,* and most recently *Acorn, The Heron's Nest,* and three HSA members' anthologies. He and Joseph Hutchison edited *A Song for Occupations: Poems about the American Way of Work,* which was published with the support of a grant from the the Colorado Council on the Arts and Humanities. He lives on a 50-acre ranch in rural Douglas County, Colorado, near Castlewood Canyon State Park, where he hikes as often as he can.

About the Calligrapher

JS Graustein has been playing with letterforms since she could hold a crayon. Now a grown up (of sorts), she is the typographer, book designer, and calligrapher for Folded Word. She collaborated with NEA Fellow William O'Daly to co-write and photograph *Water Ways*, a poetic exploration of the Granite State's blue spaces. Ecologist by training, poet by practice, and publisher by accident — she plies her trades amongst the trees in Meredith, New Hampshire. Swing on by and visit her online:

GRAYESTONE.WORDPRESS.COM

About the Press

Since 2008, Folded Word has been
exploring the world, one voice at a time
with the help of editors, authors, and readers
who value sustainable literature.

For a complete list of our titles, visit the Folded Word
website: WWW.FOLDEDWORD.COM

To report typographical errors, email:
FOLDEDEDITORS@GMAIL.COM

Want more information about our titles? Want to
connect with our authors? No problem. Simply join
us at a social media outlet near you:

- Facebook: FACEBOOK.COM/FOLDEDWORD
- Twitter: TWITTER.COM/FOLDEDWORD

FOLDED WORD IS A PROUD MEMBER OF:

Bookbuilders of Boston
Celebrating all the ways today's books are made
WWW.BBBOSTON.ORG

Community of Literary Magazines and Presses
Ensuring a vibrant, diverse literary landscape
WWW.CLMP.ORG

Folded Word reserves a portion of each print run to donate to libraries and reading programs in under-served communities. Email us at FoldedEditors@gmail.com if you would like your organization to be considered.

WHAT DID YOU THINK?

☆ ☆ ☆ ☆ ☆

Let us know with a quick rating or review at
GOODREADS.COM
or wherever you search for books.

⟞∞⟝

This title is part of the
Folded Word Special Collection
Wolfeboro Public Library
Wolfeboro, New Hampshire

Cover art, "Meditation," courtesy of Patricia Miller: PATRICIAMILLERARTLINK.COM

Cover, book, and supplemental glyphs designed by JS Graustein, featuring her Carolingian hand. Haiku were written in ink on Bienfang Graphics 360, a translucent 100% rag paper, and then digitized using Adobe Illustrator.

The title and text face is Brioso Pro, designed by Robert Slimbach in 2002, issued by Adobe Systems.

Printed in the United States of America by Walch Printing of Portland, Maine, on 70# Cougar Natural, an acid-free, FSC® Certified, SFI® Certified Sourcing, and Rainforest Alliance Certified™ sustainable paper.